PAYING BACK THE SEA

Philip Dow

Paying Back the Sea

Poems 1966-1971

Carnegie-Mellon University Press
Pittsburgh & London 1979

For my Mother & Father,

Esther Herlihy & Ralph Maxwell Dow

Acknowledgments

The author expresses thanks to the editors of the following magazines and anthologies in which some of these poems appeared:

Boundary 2: Dying; Mud; Sparrow. *Choice:* Fishing; The Life; Twilight in California. *Modern Poetry Studies:* Outskirts of Albuquerque, 1936; Sunday Afternoon Nap with My Three Years Son, Colin; This Morning. *The Nation:* Death; Self-Portrait at Thirty. *Poetry Now:* Snail. *Rapport:* Rising Early; Toad. *Transfer:* Hart Crane's Sea; Winter. *Quickly Aging Here,* Doubleday, 1969: Bats; Drunk Last Night with Friends, I Go to Work Anyway; Death; Early Morning; For a Happy Girl; The Life; Morning, in the Pastures near Suisun; Our Garden; Twilight in California. *The American Poetry Anthology,* Avon, 1976: The Duck Pond at Mini's Pasture, A Dozen Years Later; The Life; Twilight in California. *I Love You All Day,* Abbey Press, 1970: Our Garden. *Marks in Time: Portraits & Poetry,* San Francisco, Glide Press, 1968: Playing.

Further acknowledgments are due to Slow-Loris Press for publishing *Sparrow* as its broadside, no. 1, 1971; to Bread Loaf Writers Conference for a Scholarship in 1970 that honored this book while still in manuscript; to the judges for the 1967 Joseph Henry Jackson Award, who honored an earlier version, *Wishbones;* and to friends whose many acts of kindness are not unremembered.

The publication of this book is supported by grants from The National Endowment for the Arts in Washington, D.C., a Federal agency, and from The Pennsylvania Council on the Arts.

CONTENTS

PART ONE

*And a mouse is miracle enough to stagger
sextillions of infidels.*
—Whitman

The Life

Hunchbacked
by his heart
swollen with dreams
of wings, of girls whose breasts are antelope
trembling beneath the lightning
that seeds his spring: he hears the bones
of their unborn children
growing.
In his heart hut he lives,
a mute
chewing crimson flowers
to make speech, to keep
saying
    what does this do
                to save my life?

His words stall for time,
slave for the mortgage on his bones:
he knows he is the fool
who cannot solve it—
yet, goes at his heart over and over
repairing: with jellyfish, lame horses,
whistles, white cords of his body, white moths
seeking colors, damp alleys,
odors of knives,
trees, stumped, putting out tiny wings
of translucent new leaves anyway.

Listening to twilight schools of spooky minnows
tuning their scales, he has got the drift

of this night sea of star
-fish that stops all eyes:
he sees the boats go on,
overhead, with cargoes of ocarinas
and red melons—

Swimming to any shore, he finds himself
there, already, with his black horse
and his cart, heaped with salt,
paying back the sea.

Rising Early

Waking at dawn, I surprise the sea
sleepwalking through the trees,
their hovering minnow leaves. . .
a snail sails up the deep wall
of our home, raising
his frail shell—
bubble of new breath,
into faint light from another world.

Morning, In The Pastures Near Suisun

The sun gathers
last night's rain

we follow
picking mushrooms
from cowshit

Mud

This stink
dread   fishrot
rainsucked mountainsilts
duckshitted turtlebed dreck
dumb mud   that dont want to do
mothering mud
swampbottoming   makes grow
winterlong seeds frogsleep
keeps track
clots between skunk
toes   mud I can reach down elbow
in   stretch armpit deep   mud
I can Injun in
mudmask pack against chiggers
kidlike dig it   finger
and stick into dreamshape
cram holes
hold rivers   make
bricks   hutmud   I
can live in   this open
secret   mud   gives up
to sun   same
dust I am   ghosts
a windbreath   ready
to begin
again   this mud
language

This Morning

          the withered hedgerows   voluptuous
     blossomed overnight   with white
     snow
and a sparrow
          akimbo in the twiggery
     he eyes me
buff head in profile
     snub-beaked
          black line beside white over his eye
fine   filament legs sticking wide
one   head high
          the lifted leg
     showing the underbelly
             breeze riffles his down

     The hedge is alive
with him

He eyes me
     and I him

        We will not
     neither of us
          make the first move

Snail

1

I find a snail shell plugged with dirt
and hold it in the faucet's trickle
to see better its thumbskin whorl.
The dirt dissolves and some stiff dreamer begins
to swell unused muscle: garden barnacle,
one evolutionary foot
up the hope-ladder. I remember kids
pouring salt on a snail's slick hide, delighted
while it melted into slime.
And I have eaten them
with garlic and butter and wine.
I've read these night creature's horny kind
pierce each other anyplace when they mate—
every wound will yield.

Tentative on their wands, eyes appear
and probe the air—he seems to know I hold him upside down.
A shy, slender neck reaches
for anything to grip
so I touch it to my left wrist, watching its lip
(I suppose) catch
a toe-hold and roll himself slowly upright
to slide over hair and skin, shell
asway delicately with his cargo
of self, and its secretive way
of exchanging this glistening wake
for plain water.

2

Whom shall I thank for this morning?
With ribbons of spit
snails have sealed my door.

3

After Drinking Late with the Norwegian Squid

I come home with a head full
of Chippewa songs, the image of leaping Bly
in his fringed serape. The moon doesn't want my car
to make it up to the garage door
where the drifting shadows sway, dugongs
with giraffe necks and horns, camels swimming
in thick water. I get down on my knees
to shuffle the snails onto the grass,
setting them out of the headlights, hours ahead
or behind, they can't tell
they've eaten too much of the moon—
it's spilling out of them, little threads
to find their way
home by, as they must before sunrise.
The sun cooks them. I want to slide up into the pyracantha
on their lanes, and sleep with them, cold,
wet, and quiet, and let my shadow
go on back to the moon, and remember
my dad limping home drunk
one morning after a three day rain,
the snails having been washed down from their dreaming.
My dad, the lettuce lover, got down on all fours
like I am now, to cut off their heads
with his pipe knife,
humming his *rum thumb bummy nickle-o.*

Elegy

Now I lay me down
                again
   to that simple song
       you once sang
    when I was young

          words
             lost
     its tune
         remembers grief
  heart, be dumb

I've lain unable to sleep
            a long while
     as the room grew small
              around my head
        then opened
            like a tide
            my bed lost

Lay me lay me down

     now you're gone
        from your tune
   I am
     its only
        ruin

Toad

All night you *hak*
like a wino. Ahh
belly-hopper, eater
of flies—

Let me sleep
and I'll remember
you to Issa.

Without Falling

Every winter rain swells the ditches. The carp
nose in, as if it drizzled minnows.
They nose along the waterline, grazing
honeydew tendrils, watercress roots, fattening.
By July they lay, under a skein
of drying mud, like fine-veined leaves;
and whole fields of melons wild along the river, ripen
and lie rotting.

Where does love go?

Sparrow

Common as daisies, these *fader* Chaucer
(lovingly) called *sparwes*—which I mis-say
as spare wee's. I've seen these *likerous brids*,
herding the walks or blowing like leafgusts
over grasstops, furiously spin off
in pairs, screwing.
Several times today as I drove
from Sheridan to Cheyenne, they broke
my revery, spurting across
windsucked over the windshield—stupidly
me braking.

Immigrants from Britain, chosen
to harvest straw from road-apples
(my dad's word for horse dung)
they're less than useless now, pests
nesting atop drainpipes, pooping
on railings, and stinking where the family
cat hauls them beneath porches, mauls
and discards them.

My son pointing *spewwo! spewwo!*
today watching this pudgy
blackcrowned cock hover, pecking
butterflies from the grill of our parked car.
He seized the meat in his beak and shook
until the brittle wings flipped off.
I see his litter as I unpack.
Wedged beneath my luggage rack, a small female,
a spare, wee sparrow bird, dead,
falls—her little mess of dun feathers
wet, intact. If
I could put her back . . .

April

       and spring comes on.
This young girl, fingertips
holding an orange
at her new breasts, touching
elderberry trees, windows, patches
of damp soil, everything
she passes, she leaves
a delicate ache
to change; useless, full
of dreams, her hair shivers,
the orange
impatient as something she has grown.

The Duck Pond At Mini's Pasture,
A Dozen Years Later

Walking out, I flushed some meadowlarks—
Now they're down, and redwings gone into cattails.
A loose strand of barbwire begins softly thrumming.
Out over San Pablo Bay, clouds
Blow up from sunset, fading yellow
Off the Indian Tobacco.

Remembering all those nightfalls
Spent anywhere rain gathered
In corn or barley fields and ducks flew,
I hunch in pickleweed, shooting distance
From the pond, make a raspberry
With my lips and roll a whistle for Greenwing Teal
The old way learned from my brother.

Mosquitos rise out of sedge. White faces
Of Herefords bob dreamily as they graze.
In quirky teal-like flight, bats
Startle. Oil slickens my thumb on the safety
And I rub it into the marred walnut stock
Of the Winchester double, sniffing
Hoppe's lubricant, souring weeds in the flooded pond.
Behind me, darkness comes on.
A shitepoke crosses the Evening Star.

Far off, beyond the eucalyptus groves,
A pair of mallards
Cross the powerlines—
And I call, rough-voiced. They weave, dip,
Then flare. Afraid they'll pass,

I call again and my throat burns. They circle,
But I dont turn. I know to watch over water.

Out of darkness overhead, drake first,
Slowly they drop, rocking gently
On set wings, down
Slowly, into the last light—

Fishing

To Robert Hass

1

A year ago December, Bob, we met
between nightspot wharves in Sausalito
at five, paid the fifteen bucks in dark, slung
our gear aboard a party-fishing boat
Lady Luck, and cruised out the Golden Gate.

The regular Ahab crew: old Spades, Wops
and Filipinos bundled inside; beer
and jugs of dago red, penny-ante
stud. But we stuck it out on deck (poets
paying homage to *Le Voyage*) getting

our sea-legs, visions of dawn, a foretaste.
On sea otter lanes once plied by the Tsar's
fur-gorged schooners, and Spanish galleons swoll
with rawhide drums of elk tallow for Old
World lamps, we ride the Sacramento's stain

of golden sewage into played-out sardine grounds.
Whitecaps rip spindrift along our prow.
This well-wrought wood & gutteral motor
between me and fear of being eaten.
We shout, swapping our stories, or drown out.

2

An hour out we're moving with the edge
of morning
   through mists lifting
      from the first
sun touching
   ocean
     scattering petrels

avocets terns
           & murres
                whose ecologies
phase
    into waking rafts
               of buffleheads
that dive,
     or scaup and Pacific eider
echelons of pelican,
            black sea brant—
one old squaw
       singled
           from its wedge spins o
-verhead
      trying like hell to veer but
                      slip-
ping, scoters sputtering as on one
cylinder, ragging
       whitelines of spray.

Marin headlands,

      Mount Tamalpais's
female horizon. . .

3

        lone
      dorsal blades
     of primitive rock
   humped blue   Farallons
stranded twenty steep miles towards sundown

Motors cut   drifting   we
     rig up
        no talk   now   no sky
           gazing

Inverted question-marks, our spring steel hooks
rake cold flesh of old earth's sunk spine or sea's
sullen belly, our fiberglass rods throb
double, reels skreaking, our backs, shoulders, strain,
muscles bunching dense at seadrag, wrist-thews
cabling, hoisting, horsing them, three on a line
eerily played out slow-
                            ly spinning up
on sixty-pound-test gut leaders from breath
-less brine:
                deepwater blooms on a vine.
                                        Boat
lunges
        down
                trough, sidewise slides highwaved,
                                        I'm held
taut
till you man the gaff, finesse,
sway, lifting
                to this deck.

I didn't understand why
these fat orange and violet rockfish lugged
up deadweight, fightless, until I saw these
eyes. Air-pocketed, eyes popping
from sockets—
hauled from the slow kelp forests
a hundred-fifty feet underfoot, the bronze sleep
of twilight steeps, abruptly into blazing air,
gills aghast, breathing their last—
I meant *first*. I mean we buckt'm
                            in gunnysacks
pitching the undersized over
to float away
                with beercans.

Needing relief, I head for the can
stepping over a skate deflating
like a cockeyed football bladder,
pisst plumb into the sea. Got fish
smell on my private skin.

Casting again we hit the jackpot—perch
giving birth   live
spurting silverdollar size young
nothing like nestlings or pups, coldblooded
we dont hesitate using them
as bait.

4

Halfway in we leaned on the rail beside
sopped duffles of redsnappers ringperch rock
& ling cod white bass cabezone (paunched
with poisonous roe), swigging Jamaican rum
and canned coke, watching the mate clean, two
dollars a catch, hacked
                           heads jumbling
                                      like toys
through the stern chute
of Lady Luck (chuffling as a seamen
laden whore) scales trail
-ing our wake like phosphorous
sparks of the recently dead. Highpitched
gull-tattered sky. . .

We speak of fishing for rainbow trout
in the Sierras, flycasting
smooth double-tapered lines—

*I worked this one stream all day, for about two miles, trying every
fly I had. I had about two dozen, maybe more, hackles and nymphs,
wet and dry.*
   Finally I just gave up. The back of my neck was aching.

Well, I waded out to this rock, almost midstream, and had a smoke and listened to the quail calling across the hillsides.

After awhile I started daydreaming about my wife. Then, I thought of Rexroth tying a troutfly from his wife's pubic hair.

Trout had begun rising while I sat there, they were taking mayflies that were hatching and dancing in sunlight over the riffle.

I pulled some fuzz off my sweater and tied an imitation, as best I could. Damned if I didn't catch one, about eight inches. After that it came apart, but I didn't care.

Roll the trout in flour or cornmeal, salt & pepper,
sizzle in a skillet with bacon grease
until the white meat flakes free from the bones,
savoring skill not gorgeous lust.
                              Later
I'd butcher hours
spattering scales like a tide
of hate up the garage wall back of the sink
where the knife with the fishstink wooden handle
lays scabby with rust.

Buttoned high against cold and coming dark,
talking done, we ate
with fishglazed fingers, sour french rolls,
monterey jack, hard McIntosh apples. Fires
rose with the dusky coastline, marking our home.
Sawmill furnaces burning by night
where rumps of timber
are sluiced from the hills
for our Southeast Asia building boom.

We sacked
home sixty pounds each
of flesh. It was
not fishing.

PART TWO

You are a little soul carrying a corpse
—Epictetus

At the roadside
a rose of sharon—
the horse eating it
—Basho

Twilight In California

For My Father

Day of hunting done,
you find this downhill climb hardest.
But where the vineyard road begins
you balk. Breathing the good scent of sweat
and gun oil, you sit cross-legged and tense,
your hunting cap brim full of grapes;
the valley cupped below, shadowless—
waiting for the wine to be poured.
First darkness sifts out of trees into your hair.

Beyond the last ridge
your Rockies pile up,
enfolding wings, antlers,
hides of slain game
that rise, now, in twilight,
with spaniels, moving down gametrails
to drink.

At day's end
your blue eyes rust
like buckshot, changing
wine to blood.

Death

is patiently
making my mask as I sleep.
Each morning I awake
to discover in the corners of my eyes
the small tears of his wax.

When The Dead Come Home

                starlings stream
                        overhead
        a light-year
                    of collapsed stars
            of black milk

                        skywide skeins of
    the woman's hair
                    as she sings
            below the horizon
                            sings
                            over the dead
                who have gone down
                                to her
    it is her singing

                    blood gathers
                        into the sea

            to the east
                    Mount Hood
            hovers above the dusk

                    an angel
                        smouldering

Bats

Less than Angelic
Souls who evaded life
Flying in fits
Blind to Heaven's light and Earth's
They flee to an insect portion
Twisting from their echoes

Pitchpipes of grief

Insomnia

Blue veins of her breasts
and marbly scars,
scars of my animal
cruel want for her heart.

Blue veins in her breasts:
flies hugging
the nugget of meat
honed by eagles
coming faithfully.

Blue veins of your breasts,
piccolo notes or snakes:
fallible epitaphs
of the invisible artist—

Blue veins in your breasts:
wrinkly arrows pointing
nowhere, pointing here:
mottles of absence,
blue veins in your breasts.

The Shadow Of The Gate

This six foot four guy comes into the room
and throws down a sheet
of leather a sandalmaker cut
a hundred moon shaped pieces from.
It's the shadow of a gate
I've got to go through.
What do we enter into?

It's said speech sets us apart.
Our marvelous gift sinks
skyward, its beauty fastening
us to the earth.

The mule deer is crowned
by branching antlers,
that yearly fall away. Cradles
of bone.

Ode To The Soul

I go around one foot
in my life, one foot
in my death

and I dont know
in which world I'm growing.
My soul, a boot

scuffed on shale cliffs
I climb finding eggs
of vultures

that have in each yolk
a seed of my blood, that sees me:

the sea wheeling
through the sun's single lung

to fall from its shadow
like grief
again into rivers.

God disgusts me
wishing for my weakness,
the lost milkteeth of childhood.

I go around one foot
in life, one in death:
an old shoe of skin,
thick silence I move in,
taking me from this world to a next.

Song For His Silence

Say he loved the earth's blue times,
her twilight hills, and spent
his breath in the saying.
Because she was so beautiful,
and his wish fulfills: to sleep with her
and say nothing.

Sleep he desired
look for in every double moon.

His eye was a blue flower with black nothing
clenched in: The opening of a flute
squeezing air into song.

Speech flowed from his body.
Look for it then in the magpies,

Everything's all earth through
from dream into dream, the giddy dust
of breathing: look for the ecstatic worms:

These acrids tracks
of the tongue, a man like yourself

saying *The earth's blue times,*
her twilight hills,—oh, to sleep with her,

crossed
in his way
to death.

Dying

Hunting
I went into the pasture in rainstorm
sootfaced sheep fanned away
in gusts

but two
ewes balked
near a low thistled hump
a lamb lay   pewling   folded
in stupor   rainbeaten   brutish
dying

My midwinter sense
clumsy   I wanted
(to
help?)   I can't say
the staring ewes they
made me stupid

Lamb   lollheaded bleary lamb
watched me come   hitched
suddenly up   legs like sticks
tied with string

It leaned on the rain   flanks glueslick
sopped foul

as to a dog I offered my hand
for smell   I reached
to touch
those ewes broke
                    ma-a-a-a-a ma-a-a-a-a

lamb skittered
stumble-leggedly dragging
from its belly like sausage casing

                    a stringy intestine
    ma-a-a-a-a
            (O Mothers
                    your ragged griefs)
death cord
unribboned from some belly wound and

No
*Life*cord   I saw

This creature
its long joyous dying
just beginning

Outskirts Of Albuquerque 1936

         my old man closes
     his eyes and barns dismantle
             whitewash adrift like smoke
barbwire goes limp
                 unstringing fences
                     slips
                       into crevices
         roads relax
     and earth-skin stretches
                 for long breath

cottontails scoot from burrows
             come
     among pronghorns and bison
                 chasing
                     to mate

                 at the base
     of a mesa
             a young Apache sleeps
         happily in the scree
                     feeling
                 his small sagebrush fire
         hands cupping
                     between his thighs
     dreaming horses
                 horses
             many sons

From The Country

Raw morning rises
beyond a tractor sunk
to its hubs in soggy furrows.
The pale maiden of this town
is drab politics
but two young poets sweeten tea
from one's beehives
exchanging chants
about watermelons opulent as courtesans
martyred, like Indians, by history.

I've awakened to this daylight half-life
from the smiling face
of a red-haired Russian girl.
She danced for me all night—
the dawdling moon fades, but
her radiance is everywhere
rising from snow slopes
of the mountains ringing this valley town
like the steam of milk
spilling from a pail.

A mirage of bells
in the ice thaw. Blackbirds
chitter in the tules. Day
breaks, like a bubble from ice.
A plow in the sea.

for Elena Sokol

Drunk Last Night With Friends,
I Go To Work Anyway

The boss knows what shape I'm in. He tells me
about the twenties, when he was my age,
how he drank all night and woke up in strange rooms
with strange dolls. He tells me *Get lost*.

Out back, a weedbank I'd never noticed—
I head for it in cold air, remembering
dogs and cats eating grass when sick.

I sit shoulder deep in weeds. Beneath the leaves
in green air, black beetles shoulder
enormous stems, dew quivering
between stalk and leaf. In the pale moss I see
ants the size of salt grains,
and budding red flowers
smaller than these ants. A snail
dreaming in the throat of an old wine bottle.

Waiting

I lean on a flagpole,
feel a faint knocking
on my skull
& look up, the halyard
leads my eyes to the pulleys, the flag
collapsing into itself
then swirling out with the fog—
a jellyfish in surf, a
galaxy: skin-veiled vein blue,
red flushing, vibrations
buzz from the pole. Something in there.
I dont know which ear hears it.
I try the deaf one:
the pole is cold
as my bones will be. I try the other:
silence. bongggggg . . . silence
clangles. We pulse,
wind's connective tissue
entangling jellyfish in roots,
stars blind drunk, echolaliac,
in the mole's wake
as its swim honeycombs the loam
leaking the dark
that binds Orion's fiery joints
in our eyes . . .

Self-Portrait At Thirty

At last I've mastered
getting nowhere. Even my shadow
as I kill time,
comes from behind
to surpass me.
It is an awkward moment.
But I tip my hat to him,

His to me.

Early Morning

The solitary egret
in a field of new barley.

I think of the loneliness
of angels—lacking even
the body of a shadow
to share.

Aubade

a gray tom
     goes yowling
over the frost stained fence
     as though the high
knobbed testicles
         tight with spring sap
     were being squeezed
           in this cold snap

Buffalo

So cold the starlings
pair   windward on chimney
lips   Spring in the spume
pagan oracles   sing of the sooty heart

I thought the bums
at least would go south
but along Main Street I give
my change to ease
my conscience
a few red cents to the winos
and go home to feed
stale kummelweck to sparrows

I have to take off my gloves to break bread
it hurts

My eight year old calls from his window

*dont get any bread on metal
cause the birds eyes'll stick*

like this kid Wright
Morris who *thought* he knew better
than to stick his tongue
on a frozen pumphandle
or the birdwatcher
from San Rafael writing in Buffalo

luminous Pacific landscapes
while his water pipes froze
and the well gushed sludge

But he fixed them
and Morris of course loosened
his tongue

These sparrows live on hand-outs
skirting the starlings

And our other
brothers   how do they weather

The dead of winter

Winter

The willows gave up
their sensual hair
to survive this convent

Their tongues
grow bluish fuzz
and begin to forget

Their bones bleed
with the pitchblack sorrow
of crows saying midnight
midnight

So what if the stars kiss them sometimes

It's a kiss with cold teeth

Song, Or Dirge, For The Sudden Thaw

1

Some bird's bright wings flashed
just as I opened the door. No,
I didn't scare it, it was going over.
Sparrows I know at a glimpse, this
was some other wing-beat. That flicker
I'll keep in mind for the day
with the dream I better keep
secret. First thing seen
this new day. A song
chirrink   chirrink   I heard earlier.

If you dont know names
for things, listen
to them, they'll tell you
dewlark   dew lark, sing
me into morning
I'll go down from dream
into fields steaming.

2

The temperature climbed last night.
Now, dying snow
shines into streets, the sky slides
on that sheen
I walk on. Elms
leaveless as roots sticking
up from a green world
beneath, seize on the sudden thaw, blown
violent and joyous, shaking off
the cold.

The ice pack on the lake melts
along the shoreline. At edges
the wind finds voice, between
sleep and waking things
end or begin.

The cemetery snowdrifts are slumping,
gravestones uprisen again, wet in sun,
o ugly shining
in the blanched grass.
Yesterday they were nearly sunk
for good. As if a final ease
seeping up from the dead
had healed
the cuts in the stones, silencing
those anguished names,
and succeeded at last in drawing
down those grave
stones so much like stones
a man would bind
to his body
to plummet out of this world.
Grim anchors carved
with those beloved first and last possessions
our names.

Tomorrow the re-awakened will bring
shrill flowers. Even that sleep
it seems is a joke.
I'd be
that quick flickering
brightness seen first thing
today, flash
of a thistlebird,
sudden wing in sunlight.

Dew lark, to hell with secrets.
Why be ashamed we're all lost
souls, I'll tell you
my dream.

> *She was tender*
> *the fields steaming*
> *we went overfield*
> > *birdhappy in our bodies*
> *her body naked*
> > *lovely brushing mine*
> > *frost thawing*
> *on the poppies*
> > *they whished our thighs*

> *O when we joined our bodies*
> *there was light*
> > *the vein just beneath*
> *her throat skin*
> > *is blue*
> *blue as her pale eyes*
> > *her breasts burning*

I tell you it was no dream,
goddamit.
I'll look for her today anywhere, o everywhere.

4

I'm trying, dew lark, for her name.
If only, like some half-forgotten lover,
I could phone her, my voice
leaping distance
a lark saying her name
the cry of her name between us
that spark of touching.

But will she know me? I dont
even know who
I am when asleep, or waking
where I've been.

If I close my eyes . . .
No. O here
in this sudden thaw
to be shaken
like these elms
loosening from stones, dew lark
or let it be
dead.

PART THREE

*If it were sufficient to love
things would be too easy.*
—Camus

*"Lamenting" helps us to realize
our oneness with all things,
to know that all things
are our relatives.*
—Black Elk

For A Happy Girl

She is like a cricket:
singing all night

With her legs

Song For A Dutch Girl

belly   a field of ripe tulips
smoky with rainclouds
     her breasts saving
all wine
        wasted from raisins

her hands rain
         into the empty bones
    of my back

woodenshoe
     my heart
       knocks
    boatloads of horses
           storming ashore
       red horses
          breaking into rain
       blue
         chasing wings of fire

Hart Crane's Sea

This crazing lover shakes out the moon
in sparks, sings riddles from the mouths of shells,
dazzles the loveless with laving promises
of peace for pain beyond all self blame.

Crane's famished eyes drank deep this sea
and fired its veins to fathom love, flashed
up its truths like spangled flyingfish
of the dark sea's secret imaginings—

Still, loneliness deceived him. As all men,
he died before his time. But not before
he cried its heart (like a bell buoy
banging the moon) for all who drown. Always

For lovers, Crane's moondrunk music beats flames
in waves, sways bold seas of dreaming,
for sea and woman burn with the moon
and love is their tide in the blood.

for John Logan

Marriage

I tried to forget your story of chicks
leisurely fed to pet snakes (at the wake

observing your uncle). Their elastic
voluptuous mouths are made for that work
each row of teeth angled into the throat.

You also quailed telling the explorer's
odd tale of two pythons eating one shoat

until, lip to lip, one slips and devours
(also) its mate. Disturbed, I said *wouldn't you?*

Now, mad, you'd like to leave me—we've both tried.
Yet, like oysters in that Utah lab, we too
will continue waking into unseen tides.

And may yet learn the oyster's tender grace,
Yes, and secrets that ease us to say this:

It Comes During Sleep

The cry in my mouth wakes me (thirty years later)
to hear the cry is now my son's.
Dylan sleeps with a stick
in case something tries to get
into his bed. I go to his room, listening
to the rain
raining on the roof, and pull the covers over him.

I used to get up about this time and walk
miles in the rain, duckhunting
with my father—he's an old man now, far away,
dying year by year
of lung disease. He smokes
most of the night, alone,
telling the same old hunting stories.

Is this the dream that wakes us?

Our Garden

My love sometimes makes her shrill.
I've imagined leaving her and our sons
for the life I deserve
and should have had ten years ago
(and wasn't ready for).

Tonight the four year old jumped in the tub
clothes and all
to wrestle me,
we helped his little brother in.
We laughed and she mopped the floor.

I know they owe me nothing,
demand everything,
and trust.

And I could never understand
how a man could prune his tree
in hope of greater yield.

Sunday Afternoon Nap
With My Three Years Son, Colin

1

my forearm
beneath his head
begins buzzing
& I drift
along its hide
leaking
into sleep

light drowsing
out of my eyes
my feet like slow fish
float
twitch
in their wake
my legs rippling
away & I pour
into dream
or the soul
flows back into my body

2

Below the headland
on the gully trail, I began to slide
on the blue, flaking shale—
Dad, gripping my arm, lifted me
easily down
onto the shelf
of sea grass glistening
in the fissured rock along the edge
of the minus tide's
slack sea-licks.

Blackcapped gulls   overhead   lazed
open-armed in contours of mist
flowing up the bluff
crying   *kelp   kelp*

Dad climbed
between rocks   dripping
surfswells washing
through purple and white musselbeds.
I tagged behind, watching small red crabs
sidling into crevices.

In a heap of slick kelp
stinking in the sun, I slipped
falling face down
into its tangled strips of coppery hide.
Reaching for a hold
on a rock's cusp
with my scraped hand, I poked
my fingers in a plump anemone's orange skin
exposed like living pulp
of this undersea rock.
It puckered
from my touch, shading
to crimson, spraying brine
that stung my hand.

Oh, Sonnybuck, Dad called,
look what's here.

He stood inside the shade of a cave
uncovered by low water,
and I crossed to him
feeling every slimey thing underfoot
alive.

See here.
Breathing moist decay
I stared into the dark
as he poked this sac
of a thing   slung
inside the cave's lip,
a dusky octopus
the size of a man's head.
Each warty tentacle leeched
tight to its fix, sucking
the rockside with its string of mouths.

Dad pried his abalone iron
under and tugged
stripping one sucker
after another, resticking
till he quit.

            It dropped then

        plumbskinned, stunned in light
                tumbling
writhing
              for the sea
& Dad snagged a leg
             slinging
it up
   one of its snakes
coiling his arm

   arm swarming
my pulse   eating
my pulse
     eating me

3

My son beside me turns
his sweat face
into my breath
hot stinking feast
of raw meat
            his used breath
clogging into my lungs

I feel
      he chewed
his way out
through my ribs
                  while I slept

      In my child's breath
I face
            into my death

Mother

I awoke hot, startled in daylight, calling
you: ashamed: black waters were streaming over
faces, shell-blue fungi on fallen maples,
trestles in crumbling

fires collapsed: kingfishers above, my children
yelling *Mom, wake Daddy, I caught a big one:*
oh, so that's who you are, my Mother: *Mother:*
Father's-old-widow.

November

for Colin's birthday

This is the month my father died
the same month he was born
it's not a matter of manly pride
I've nothing left to mourn

I mourned myself when I was a child
because he was too strong
and later when I had grown so wild
I thought him always wrong

Early I loved him as a god
with love that breeds its hate
because no father survives a god
I almost learned too late

This is the month my father died
the month my son was born
like every father broken by pride
I've everything to mourn

I thought I'd mourned it all and more
as my father's son
but sons grow up as fathers before
I'm fathered by my son

I say what every father has said
though he spoke it to none
these words that mourn the live and the dead
son and father and son

Playing

1. *Eyes Closed*

My kid says *I*
hope I die soon
so I'll be an angel
and leans sidewise

Sun catching
me wide-eyed

Not as it slides
beneath the eyelids
of the peach
sunspots changing
to sugar

It's eaten
by a darkness inside
me   the pit
at my core
waiting

2. *Eyes Open*

This morning's poem   hand
written on a long
sheet of rice paper   I rolled
like a spyglass
to look at this
child
giggly Colin
three year old   leans
sideways
to look back

How a poem may join
us eye
and eye
with joy

Hot Day Early In Spring

The colt's jubilance. Three roans flopped
in the sun. This time
too early for flies
lovely for them—all summer
they'll have to sleep standing up, standing
paired, sweeping tails
in their mate's face.

I am so lonely for her this morning
when I read aloud those words
asked by a wine loving man
ten hundred years ago   *Who in spring*
                          can bear to grieve alone
their vinegar dries my mouth.

Wildflowers smear the deep meadows
with lush hues and visibly thicken
the air with their odorous pollens.
The hillslope grasses already burnish
gold. These cannot long distract me.
The seven month
dry summer gathers in the dust.

The fly's life span
like his heart and wing beat
how it must blur
in his bundles of separate eyes
only his eggs surviving winter.
Horses
all winter standing
stupidly in the rains.

Your Voice Of Bees-Birdpsalms-
Meadowfeathers-Me-You

calling me to these hills
these fields you say *do not enclose us*
they shed all light like joy
(these voluptuary hills where cloud-shadows
in their passing smeared winter investitures
foretastes of green uprisings, these emerald
eruptions into sun
wed dream and doing as they come)
this is the country of the heart

you run thigh-deep
into the hayslope nebulae
of meadowfoam scattering
bees pollen ripples
of larks flying
your hair
as you turn I catch
your hands and we spin
stagger-dancing into lark
loud circles, senses giving in
to the earth's heady pull
spilling backflat breathless together
vision blurring ringed round with indian clover
surfs of lupine shooting stars red
giants white dwarf morning
glory wheeling
foxtails and dewdazzled poppies dizzying
earthwings suspending us
forever above this ringing deep spring
blue well
of the sky

You Are Brushing Light From Your Hair

my voice is a hand
each sound a finger
tender in its need
to touch you
deeply where no hand
touches ever

Green Wine

I dont believe in God either . . . in your eyes
a faint rinse of wine
and crying risk your disguise,
feeling solace I'd offered your pain
opened mine.

Maybe that's as much help as we can hope to give—
only admit Joy,
a fugitive emotion,
& a man in lucid moments
goes on cursing God
for his infliction: Love.

So you asked me for a poem.
If that eased hell in the heart
why'd Berryman jump his bridge to die?
Poetry.
Men die miserably everyday for the lack of what's found there.
Do we feed ourselves a pack of lies
or how many times do we die also
of what is found there?
Somebody'll never hurt you anymore!—
that maggot, self-pity.
Was I so corpse-rehearsed I couldn't spit?

Green wine. Dont ask. Too much new
to be forgotten before words you ask for ripen.

Your garden, if you succeed with snails
I'm glad you dont harm
though they've left their death-scribble
on the tomato leaves.

Begin early
stake your tomatoes with willow switches
they'll bud pussy willows
sing to the tendrils tenderly
there's no recipe but cooking and eating with those you love
or not at all
& when you cook remember
Li Po said *a cup of wine*
levels life and death.

The empty country highway soars
above the Petaluma River
so you see steeply the stars
have failed with the darkness.

I dont know Berryman.
Pitch dark maybe, stars.gone out of the heart,
maybe to stay at such height.

Dim land unmingles
umbers and russets
insinuating first light
sky returning the river
snail's trace

wings in faintest green
wings in the waking barley
cry themselves out   *ker loo*
                ker loo   ker loo
—morning words

I'll give you: this day
from this my life
these few green words